this is how

you know

i want you.

for Pel ♡

*sending you
so much love always.*

AVA.   ◁AVA.

copyright © 2015 victoria nguyen.

all rights reserved.

no part of this book may be reproduced in whole or in part, or stored in a retrieval system, or transmitted in any form or by any means, electronic, mechanical, photocopying, scanning, recording, or otherwise without permission from the writer.

ISBN-10: 1515306399
ISBN-13: 978-1515306399

some people are so deep
you fall into them
and you never stop falling.

this is for you.

april 2, 2013.

this is the night we met.

it felt like something important.
it felt like my whole life was about to start.

i have felt this way a few times,
but the feeling never stays.

you tell me:
i'm allowed to feel anything i want
just never for forever.

*i may have given you too much importance,
but this is how you know i want you.*

*you came in slowly like the fog
and consumed me.*

april 2, 2013.
8:42 pm

i am at another party i do not want to be at.
i am standing
and i am blending in with the wall.
jason is being an asshole again
and his girlfriend's about to cry.
tomorrow, they won't remember
and tomorrow, they won't care.

i see you
but i try not to see you.
you see me
and i feel seen.

i want you.
i want you.
i want you.

that is all i see in your eyes.

april 2, 2013.
8:50 pm

you came up to me
or i came up to you,
i can't remember.
but i think you came up to me.

you told me the truth
and i never heard anyone
tell the truth so easily before.

more importantly,
you didn't try to touch me.

you were just trying to be you.
and i know how hard that is,
but you were doing it so well.

you were so real
i was afraid to touch you,
so i didn't.

we were surrounded by plastic and gloss
and somehow, you survived,
and i just want to be next to you
and not touch,
for as long as i can.

april 2, 2013.
9:12 pm

i am sitting
and you are sitting with me.
this is new
and i am nervous.

nervous that this will not go anywhere.
nervous that this will go too far.

i think i love you.
i think this is possible.

you are sitting next to me, so close,
i feel fire and all i want to do is tell you,
i love you.

it's taking everything i have to stop myself
from doing that, to keep those three words
tucked neatly beneath the tongue and out of
light.

i get up and move myself across the room
and i can feel your eyes burning holes into
the shape of your irises behind my ears.

i clutch my drink and chase the three words
down to my liver.

i love you
and i am a terrible pretender.

april 2, 2013.
11:29 pm

at one point,
you moved your hand over my leg.
you squeezed it a little
and i felt warm all over my body.

at one point,
everyone around us
got a little drunker
and everyone around us
started to fade away.

your hand.
my leg.
one thing between.

april 3, 2013.
12:56 am

i didn't want to seem too eager.
i went to go look for my friends.
i couldn't find any of them.
so, i went for a drink instead.

i found you asleep on a blue couch.
i sat down beside you
and you opened your eyes,
took one look at me,
and wrapped your arms around my neck.

you pulled me down close to you
and you kissed me.

you tasted like
christmas morning
high on cocaine.

at the party,
you had been drinking and
you fell asleep.

i sat down beside you and
you opened your eyes and
you pulled me down close to you
and it was never close enough.

april 3, 2013.
7:44 am

i woke up on a friend's couch.
we woke up early
because i had to get my car.
parking in the city always sucks.

i asked her what happened last night.
she told me i disappeared.
she told me i was with you.
she told me i looked happy.

*i don't remember much from last night
aside from your eyes
and how they never left mine.*

sexts:

'i want you
to take off more—
not just your clothes.'

'don't look at me.
i feel naked
when you stare.'

'hungry?'

i fill up with questions.
i always think the worst.

did i text back too soon?
am i too much?

everything is fragile.
distance, too delicate.

ridiculous—
how timing can ruin everything.

how much is too close
before i'm smothering you?

how much is too far
before you forget i exist?

i question everything
and that is why
i'm still alone.

april 5, 2013.

you called me.
you want to see me.

i was worried because i don't remember
what you look like,
but i am more worried you remember
what i look like.

i am worried that
you will change your mind.

i am awkward on the phone.
i tell you i am awkward everywhere.

i swear i knew your voice
before i ever even heard it.

you sounded like home.

april 9, 2013.

i am eating.
i am thinking of you.

i swallowed
the syllables of your name
and i was full.

april 10, 2013.

me and you are at a friend's apartment.
we're doing blow
and drinking jameson.

we're looking at websites
that we think are beautiful.

we are talking
and i'm hoping i will not forget.

the sun's coming up,
and it's burning through the windows.
i have work tomorrow
so we go to sleep.

i'm trying to sleep,
but my heart is beating so fast
and i can't tell if it's because
of you or the blow.

but it's beating
like a drum going to war
and i think it knows—
    you are near
    and you could be closer.

april 15, 2013.

it's still new.
i'm still worried about a lot of things.
i am too much in my head.

you tell me it's okay to be afraid.
you tell me you're afraid too.

i just wanted you
to sink your hands into me
and turn on everything
i turned off feeling
for the world.

i wanted you
to make me feel again.

my hope of all hopes
is that your touch
has the power to burn my flesh
down to the truth of my bones,
and i will finally know
what being touched means.

i imagine your hands, so warm,
my heart will believe it is spring,
and my heart will bloom wide open for you.

*i want so much
to touch you
where my hands cannot.*

april 17, 2013.

i fell hard.
you fell fast.

we knew of no other way to fall.

you are the fresh scar
  upon my heart,
 the new slit
   where love
      finds its way through.

april 20, 2013.

i am sitting in the sun.
i am falling asleep.
i take a drag.
i dream of you.

of your hands.
your lips.
your eyes.

everything.
everything.
everything.

i imagine your hands
and my body becomes
a mountain blooming with wild flowers.

i imagine your mouth
and my body becomes
a juicy, round peach in june.

i imagine your eyes
and my body becomes
a web of burning stars.

i imagine your soul
and my body becomes
naked before you.

april 21, 2013.

in this very large house
is a very large room
with a very large space
between you and me.

space is important to me,
but not here.
not now.
not between you and me.

*every choice i have ever made
after you existed
has been dependent on exactly
how close i can have you next to me
and how long i can get you to stay.*

your tongue on my tongue

like honey
like silk
like sky
like skin
like soft
like hard
like rain

your hand in my hand.
   fingers—
      in and out,
      and in between.
your skin on my skin,
   an electric new thing.

this is what i want.

all i wanted was your hair on my face.
  black streaks
    over my eyes,
    on my mouth,
  an electric purr against my skin.

your flesh wet
  and sticking next to mine.
your body with my body,
  i kiss.
  i kiss.
  i kiss.

i adore you,
you radical thing.

april 26, 2013.

you tell me the places
that formed you,
of where you've been.
places that touched you first,
before me.

i drew lines
between the marks
freckled on your skin.

i imagined i drew maps
of every space
you've ever been.

places i've never been to.
places where you belonged.

places to drive everywhere,
all over you,
all night long.

april 27, 2013.

i asked you to say something
in your mother tongue.
you tell me that
you don't have the accent down.
i tell you i have the same problem.

you gained courage.
you told me your name
and i never heard anything
more fucking beautiful.

do not speak to me
   in the language we both know.
i want to feel your native tongue
   and where it came from.

   i want to know where you begin.

a terrifying thought
uncurls and straightens itself
inside my mind:
                        what if i love you?

you are an earthquake,
        a sudden thing.
you move and my body shakes.
you speak and i tremble.

you are a mountain,
        a stunning thing.
you are the sand
     that's against the grain.
  you stand and i stumble.

april 29, 2013.

we don't have a lot of time.
we make do.

5 minutes here.
28 minutes tomorrow.
one hour now.

you are the slow hand over my lips,
the sex of my flower.

you are the day stain in my hair,
the white in my night.

the perfect hour.

may 1, 2013.

my insecurities are getting the best of me
and i want to give my best to you.

but sometimes
i am too much in my own mind.

i make up something.
i push you away.
and i hope you don't change your mind.

i want to give you all of me,
but i'm scared you want more
   than what i have to give.

may 5, 2013.

i'm sorry.
i don't really know
how to be with another person.
this is all so new to me.

i tend to destroy things i'm afraid of.
i tend to destroy things that i love.
 things i don't believe i'm deserving enough.

i am broken
and i hope you can understand.

may 6, 2013.

you told me to take more time.
you wanted me to be sure.

you told me that your love will be here,
that you could never be far from me.

gravity won't let you leave.

i do not care if you tear me apart.
that is the only way
i know how to let you in.

may 7, 2013.

i told you to come in.

i am sure.
i don't care about anything else anymore.

i want you.

*let your love cover me like skin.
i want the whole world to see.*

may 8, 2013.

you touch me.
i feel it everywhere.

you touch me
and all i have are questions—
a million things i don't understand.

you touch me
and i no longer care.

when you touch me,
it is both heavy and light.
and if you feel me
like i feel you,
you would question
everything and nothing
and still, somehow,
be at peace.

may 10, 2013.

my room is dark.
i don't like to let the light in.
but the little light that does come in
always finds its way to you.

i watched you undress
   as i always do.

a stray light fell
   and found its home
   in the nook
      of your shoulder.

i go to kiss it
   and welcome it home.

june 6, 2013.

it's june.
you are still here.
beside me.

you are waiting for me at the table.
you are reading something.
you are always reading something.
i hope you're re-reading something
i wrote to you.

i take a breath.
it's not a dream.

this is hard for me to understand.
i have never really felt this way before
and i can't really explain how i feel.

i try so hard not to think about you,
not to bring you up in every conversation,
not to be one of those people
who can do nothing
but talk about someone they love.
—*i'm obsessed.*

i found you or you found me
and i can't help it
and i've stopped caring,
you make me so happy.

i expected nothing
and you became everything
and this is hard for me to understand.
i have never really felt this way
and i can't really explain how i feel,
i just feel like for the first time ever,
everything here is enough.

june 13, 2013.

i pay attention to you
more than i pay attention to anything.

everything you do is infectious.
everything you do is new to me.

how can someone's laugh be so
lovely and different every single time?

earlier,
when you held my hand at the theater,
i found a new scar
and you leaned in and told me:
   it doesn't hurt anymore
      and it will never hurt again.

i'm so hooked
on how your mind works,
on what you notice,
on everything that excites you.
i'm so caught up in
how you see the world,
how you see everything
and still offer up your love
for all to take it.

you give me a glimpse of your heart
and i can't tell you
how much you turn me on.

june 17, 2013.

you tell me i am enough.
i have always been enough.
i have always been more.

i tell you
    as long as i am enough for you,
    i'll be okay.

you are in everything that remains.
  inside.
  outside.

there is not much of me left,
but whatever's left
belongs to you.

.

there is a comfort in you
i've never known.
when i am with you,
i am at rest.

july 4, 2013.

i knew i really loved you
when i didn't care whether or not
you were with me.

i only wanted you to be happy.
i wanted you to be free.

the entire sky exploded into fireworks
and you were with me.
we were laying in the grass
and the sky was falling into our hair,
it felt incredible
because we were together

because we wanted to be.

i have no desire to own you,
to claim you.
i love you just as you are.

free.
your own.

i just want to be near you.
to love you.
to be with you,
as much as you will allow.

this
is
what
happens
when
i
say
your
name.

i say your name
   and flowers fall from my mouth
    and fall into yours,
   and you tell me
    i taste like spring,
     like a new day
      with hints of honey,
       a bit like chocolate with chili.

you say my name
   and fireworks of wildflowers
    bloom mad in the sky
   and a garden grows wild in my heart.

july 29, 2013.

waking up used to be hard.

waking up to the same bullshit—
   day in.
   day out.
makes you feel
something not human.
something no one cares about.

i wasn't really living before you,
but i can't wait to wake up now.

i can't wait to start the day
and open my eyes
and see you.

my stretch marks—
    like streaks,
    like milky way.
you stare at them
    like you stare at stars.

come closer
    and lose yourself in me.

i open for you
  like a flower.
i let you in
  like a new day.

you speak and
i want to wrap my legs
around your mouth
and let my love cover
your honeyed tongue.
you speak and
the want blooms
ripe round inside me.

this
is
what
happens
when
you
say
my
name.

i can think of nothing
but your mouth
and the way you say my name—
   how it falls off your tongue
     and falls into everything
       that i am,
      changing the weather inside me.

   i am a hot, burning summer,
     a wild blooming of wild flowers,
      a storm of skin and bones
        by the way you say my name.

august 8, 2013.

i think about you too much.
i know it isn't healthy,
but i know you do the same.

somehow,
for now,
i think this makes it okay.

i need something to do
to keep my mind off of you.

    what else could i find here
    that i will love enough
    to ruin me?

i wanted to destroy you.

you are mine to ruin.
something so beautiful
should only exist for me.

august 10, 2013.

i start missing you
the second before you leave.

i think whatever this is
is enough to undo me.

i want to go back to that morning
where we blacked out all the windows
  and we woke up
    tangled in each other's others.
      a bedlam of
      limbs, skin,
      hair, lips—
        complicated by love
          or other drugs.

i miss you.
i am homesick for you
and this is new for me.

    there is a want,
    and there is a you,
    and there is a me.

the need in you
   is the need in me,
and it is soft and heavy,
like rain clouds unable to empty.
   like rain clouds, so full—
      the entire sky turns black.

august 17, 2013.

i hate how mortal we are.

i hate how we're going to
rot and decay
and return to the earth
as these tragic and fragile things.

i hate that nothing lasts forever,
and i hate that this is what gives
    everything meaning.

tell me we won't get used to this.
to this sad life.
this wrecked existence.
tell me you're not miserable.
that you love me.
that your life is here with me.
tell me of future plans,
of storms that may happen.
tell me how you're scared
and that this comforts you.
tell me i'm your sky,
but i'm too blue for you.
tell me something different.

tell me something i will not know.

we talk of plans

  that are going to happen.
we talk of the future,
   as if we know we will last.

there is a sort of comfort in that.

i don't tell you i love you, but i do.
and you know,
because of how i look at you.
you know you are wanted by me.
that i want to be near you,
close to you.
so close—
   you take in air,
   and it is i
        who comes alive.

september 1, 2013.

i love how it feels to be with you,
like you fit into me
and i fit into you.

i love how easily
i fall asleep
when i'm with you.

come.
i know you're tired.
use my breasts as your pillows.
    let the hum of my heart
    seduce you to sleep.

i weave little flowers
into the silk of your skin.
i kiss little dreams
into the milk of your eyes.

— *before you sleep.*

go to sleep.
dream of me.

AVA. currently lives in california and is thinking about what she wants to eat next.

instagram: @VAV.AVA

Made in the USA
Columbia, SC
07 December 2017